LET'S CALCULATE WORK!

PHYSICS AND THE WORK FORMULA

PHYSICS FOR KIDS – 5TH GRADE

CHILDREN'S PHYSICS BOOKS

Speedy Publishing LLC

40 E. Main St. #1156

Newark, DE 19711

www.speedypublishing.com

Copyright 2017

In this book, we're going to talk about how work is calculated. So, let's get right to it!

WHAT IS WORK?

We use the word "work" all the time to represent effort that we make.

Getting an A on your physics test might be considered work. Pushing a large rock from one point to another point might be considered work. Holding a brick over your head in one position might be considered work. Even reading this page might be considered work. However, in all these examples only one of them is considered work in the subject area of physics.

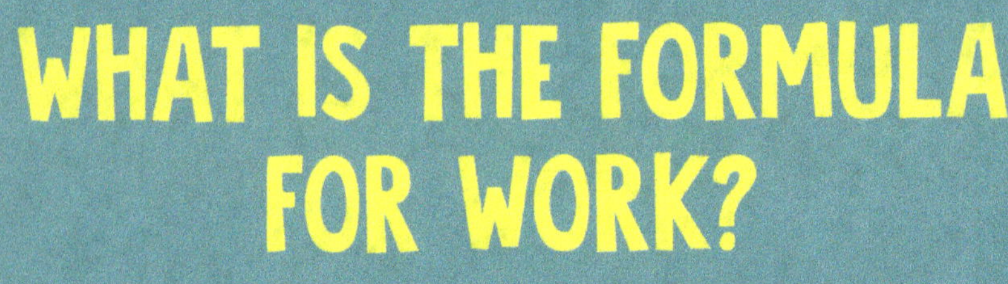

WHAT IS THE FORMULA FOR WORK?

In physics, only the example where we are pushing the rock would be considered work. That's because in physics the definition of work is when a force acts upon an object and that force causes the object to be displaced from its beginning point to a point away at its ending point.

In fact, if you pushed and pushed and pushed until you were blue in the face and the rock didn't move at all, this wouldn't be considered to be work, in physics. You'd be tired and would have exerted a lot of effort, but it wouldn't be considered work.

There's a very simple equation to calculate work in physics, it is:
Work equals the force exerted times the displacement

In symbols, this equation is $W = Fd$, where W represents work, F represents force, and d represents the displacement of the object.

This formula works when the force and displacement are going in the exact same direction.

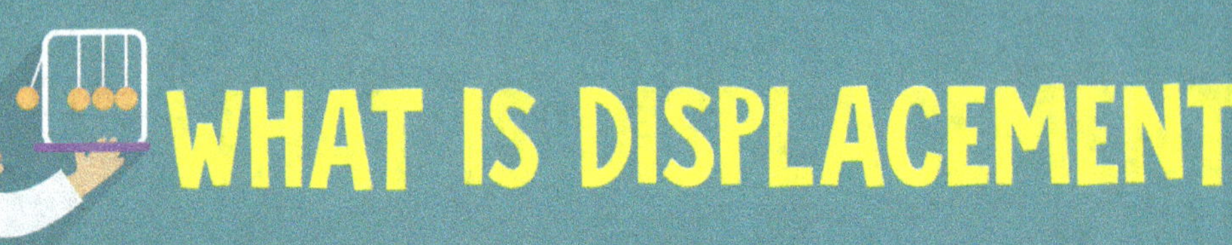

WHAT IS DISPLACEMENT?

In order to understand the work formula for physics, it's important to understand what displacement really is. It's a vector quantity, which simply means that it represents the direction of a movement. The most important concept to remember is the starting point and the ending point are the most critical pieces of information to determine an object's displacement.

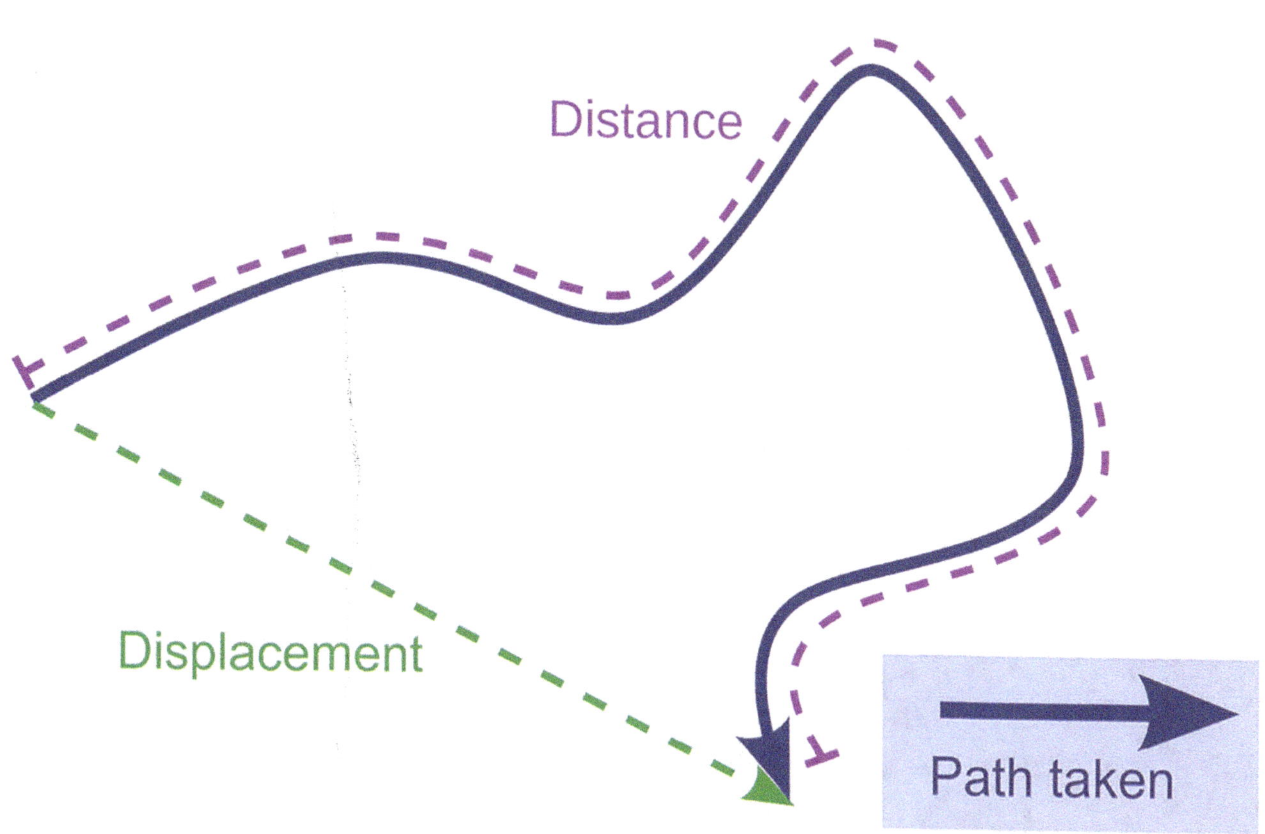

Distance
Displacement
Path taken

et's look at some examples.

Suppose you're a runner and you're running on a circular track. Let's say you start at Point A on the track and you run all around the track and now you're back at Point A again. You can run and run and run on the track but if you end up back at Point A you won't do any "work" as defined in physics because you are in the same place you were when you started.

So, in other words, to have zero displacement, you or the object in question must have a starting point and an ending point that are the same.

The same thing happens when you are traveling in a straight line. If your school bus takes off from point A and then gets to point B it has a displacement, but if it starts at point A and returns to point A then it has a displacement of 0, which will mean there's no "work" involved. Zero displacement will always result in zero work.

SCHOOL BUS

Finally, let's look at an example of throwing a ball in the air. If you throw a ball up and it comes down in the exact same spot you threw it from, then there is zero displacement. No work has been done.

If you held a box up in the air, that requires effort on your part, but if the box doesn't move anywhere, then no work has happened. However, if you raise the box up to put on the shelf, then work has happened because the box has been displaced.

HOW IS WORK MEASURED?

The standard unit that is used for the measurement of work is the joule. It's equivalent to the newton-meter. The units used to measure work are the same as the ones used to measure units of energy.

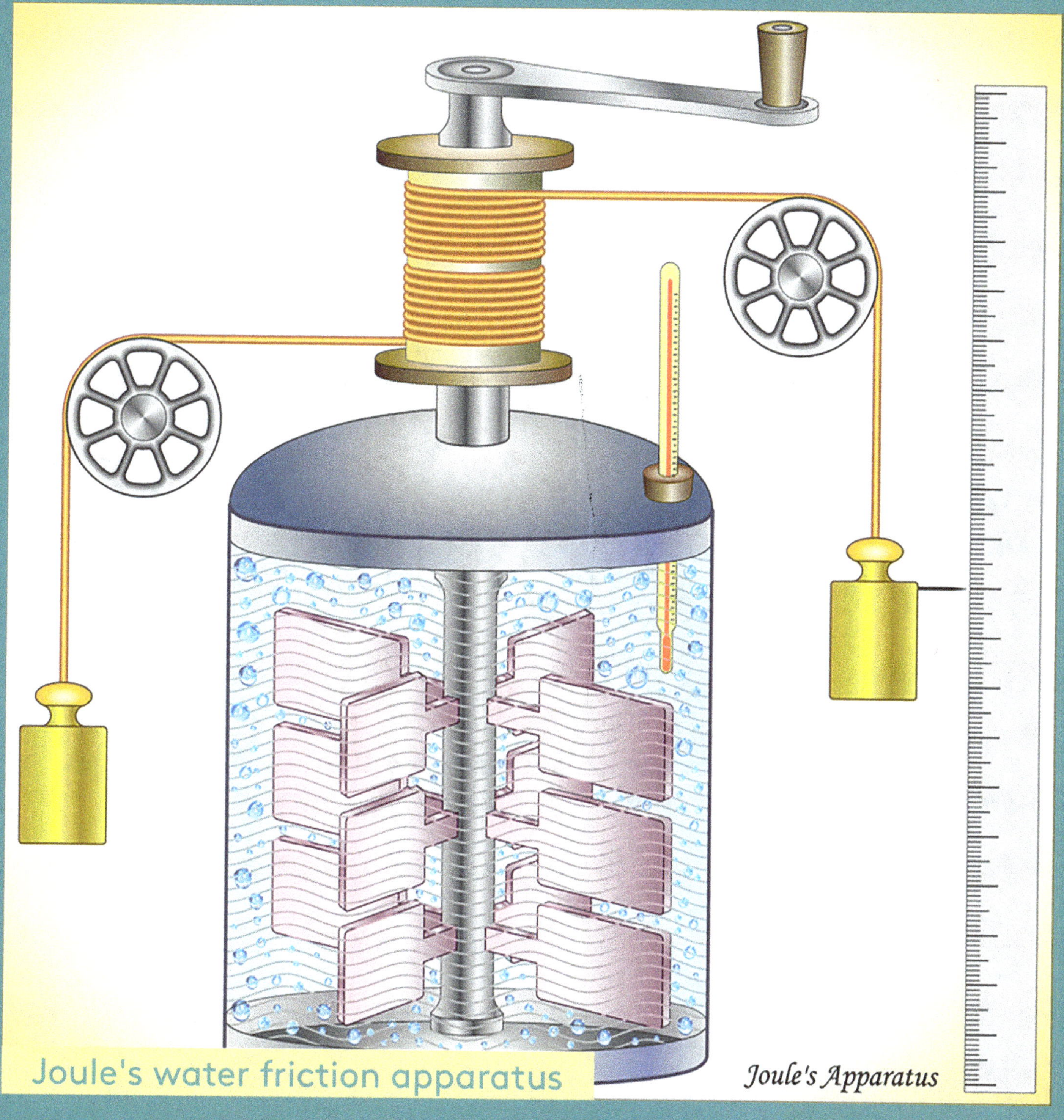

Joule's water friction apparatus
Joule's Apparatus

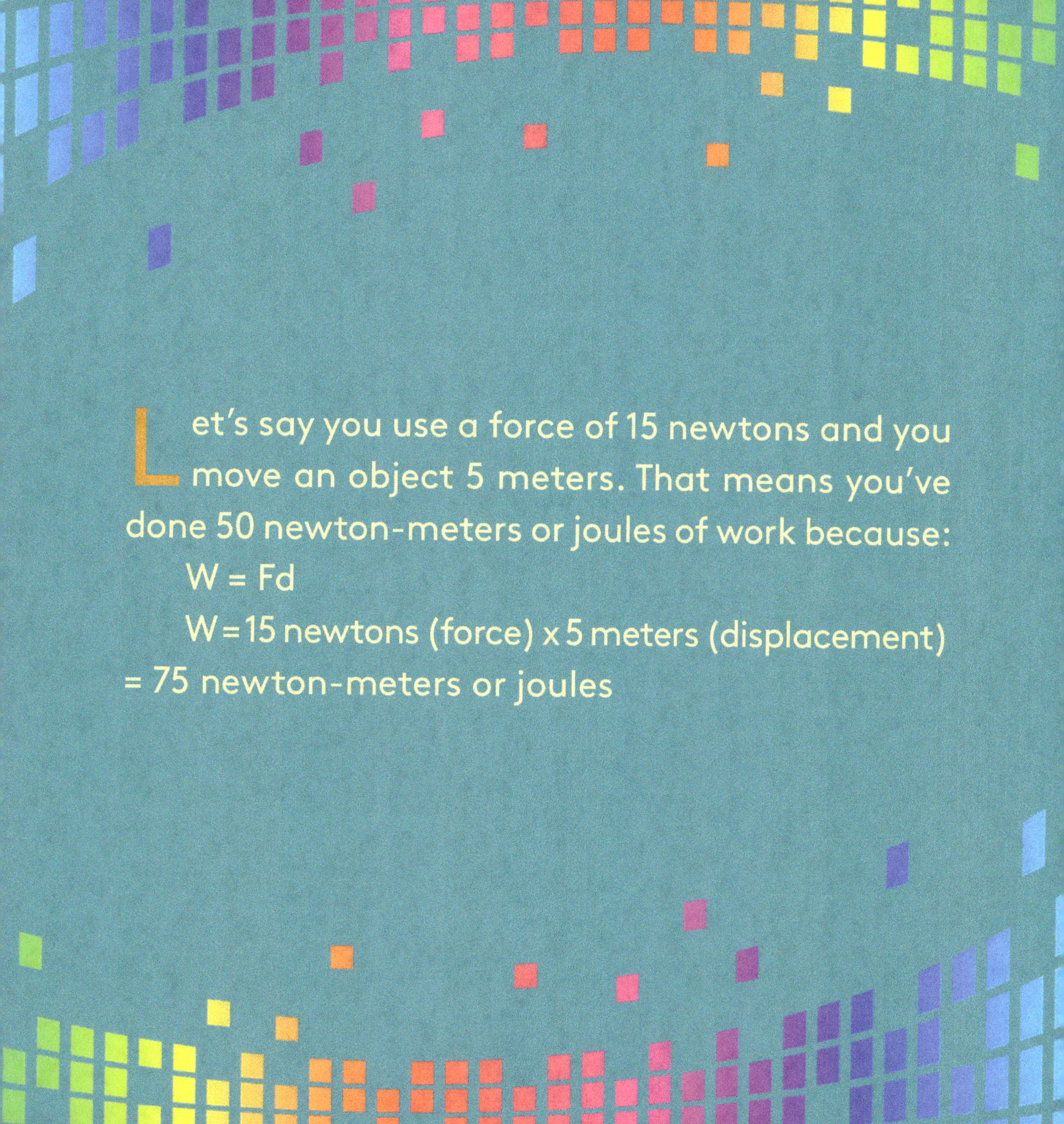

Let's say you use a force of 15 newtons and you move an object 5 meters. That means you've done 50 newton-meters or joules of work because:

W = Fd

W = 15 newtons (force) x 5 meters (displacement) = 75 newton-meters or joules

But, what is a newton exactly? A newton is named after the great physicist Isaac Newton. It's one of the International System of Units (SI). It's the force that's needed to accelerate an object that has a mass of one kilogram at the rate of one meter per second squared. The object is moved in the direction that the force is applied.

Isaac Newton

orce is a vector and so is displacement, but work is scalar, which simply means it doesn't have a direction. It's just a magnitude, which is a size or quantity as measured in joules.

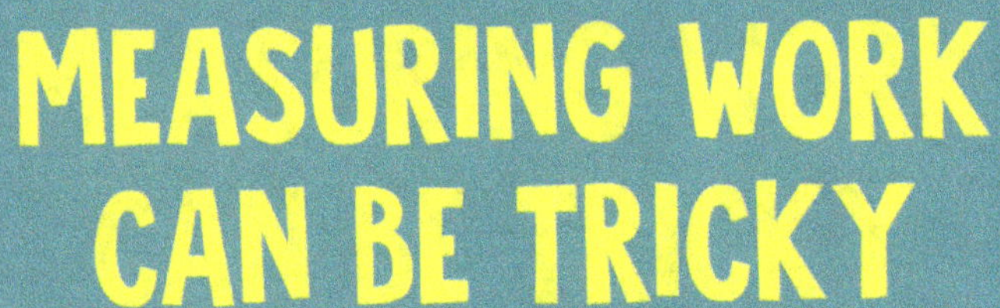

MEASURING WORK CAN BE TRICKY

When you are solving problems involving the formula for work, you need to identify the force that's actually causing the displacement. For example, if you are driving a car, you aren't the force. You're just steering it. The force is the engine that is driving the car.

HERE ARE SOME OTHER EXAMPLES TO UNDERSTAND WORK

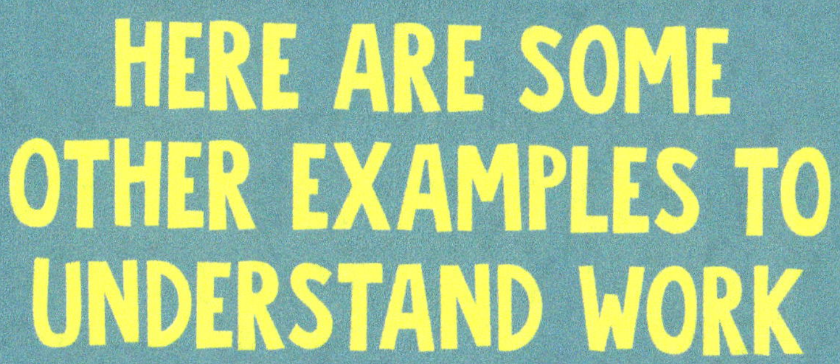

f you pushed on prison bars, but no matter what they didn't move, then no work has occurred. The bars weren't displaced so no work has happened and you're still in jail!

If a man is holding a heavy box over his head in one position and is walking westward across a huge field, then no work has happened. That's due to the fact that the force and the displacement are not happening in the same direction. The force in this case is the man lifting the box into its vertical position. It's a vertical movement. The displacement is a westward movement so the directions are not the same.

If you drop your pencil and it falls and hits the ground, then work has happened. The displacement from your hand might be about 1 meter or about 3 feet and the direction of force is the same vertical direction. The force acting on the pencil to make that displacement happen is gravity!

A SPECIFIC EXAMPLE OF CALCULATING WORK

Andy is mowing the lawn for his grandmother. Unfortunately, she has a push mower. That means the mower doesn't have an engine and the grass is cut as Andy pushes it. This is going to mean a lot of hard work for Andy.

You'll be able to calculate the work Andy does if you know how much force he uses, whether there is a displacement of the mower, and whether the force he's applying is in the same direction that the mower is moving. Let's say he's using 100 Newtons of force and the displacement of the mower is 205 meters as he cuts the grass.

Before you can solve this problem you have to ask yourself these questions.

Is Andy really pushing the mower himself? The answer is yes, because there isn't a power motor in this mower.

Is the mower moving? The answer is yes. It travels or is displaced 205 meters.

Is the force Andy is applying in the same direction as the mower is displaced? The answer is yes. He's pushing it forward and the mower is being displaced in the same direction.

So, now we can calculate the work that Andy has done.

W = Fd

W = 100 newtons x 205 meters = 20,500 N • m or newton-meters or joules

CALCULATING FORCE OR DISPLACEMENT WHEN WORK IS KNOWN

After Andy finishes mowing the lawn he pushes the mower to the garage, which is over 30 meters from where he was on the lawn. He does over 3000 joules of work. How much force did he have to use to get the mower to the garage?

Force = Work ÷ displacement

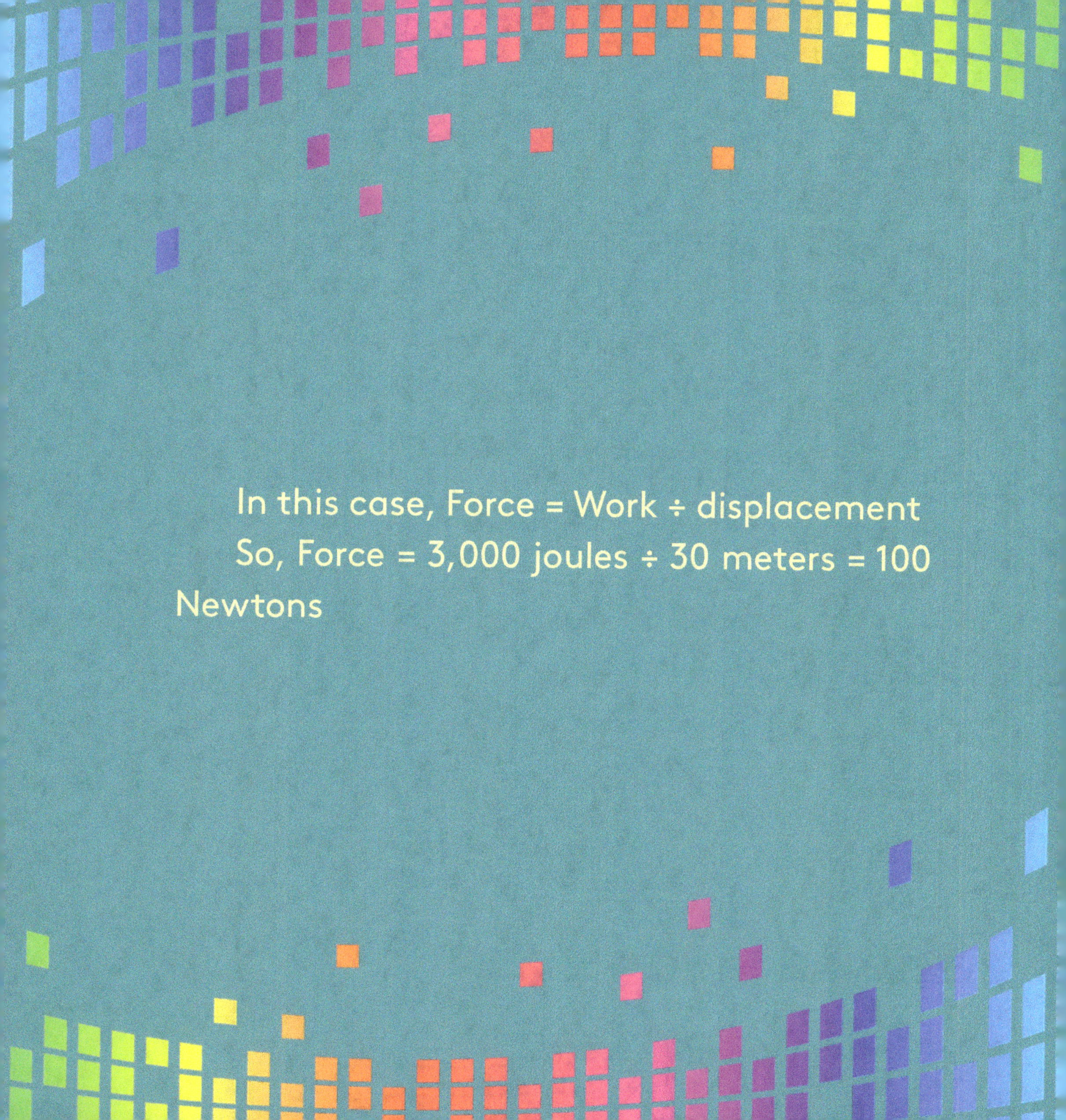

In this case, Force = Work ÷ displacement
So, Force = 3,000 joules ÷ 30 meters = 100 Newtons

MORE WORK PROBLEMS

Sometimes the angle between the force and an object's displacement is neither 0 degrees nor 90 degrees. Then a slightly more complicated formula needs to be used.

Force = 3,000 joules ÷ 30 meters = 100 Newtons

W = F x d x cos theta or
W = F x d x cos θ

he formula includes the angle that occurs between the direction of the force and the object's displacement. The angle measurement is represented by the Greek letter theta.

W = F x d x cos theta or W = F x d x cos θ

For example, let's say you have a rock on an incline. The force that is working on the rock is gravity, which is vertical, straight down to the center of the Earth.

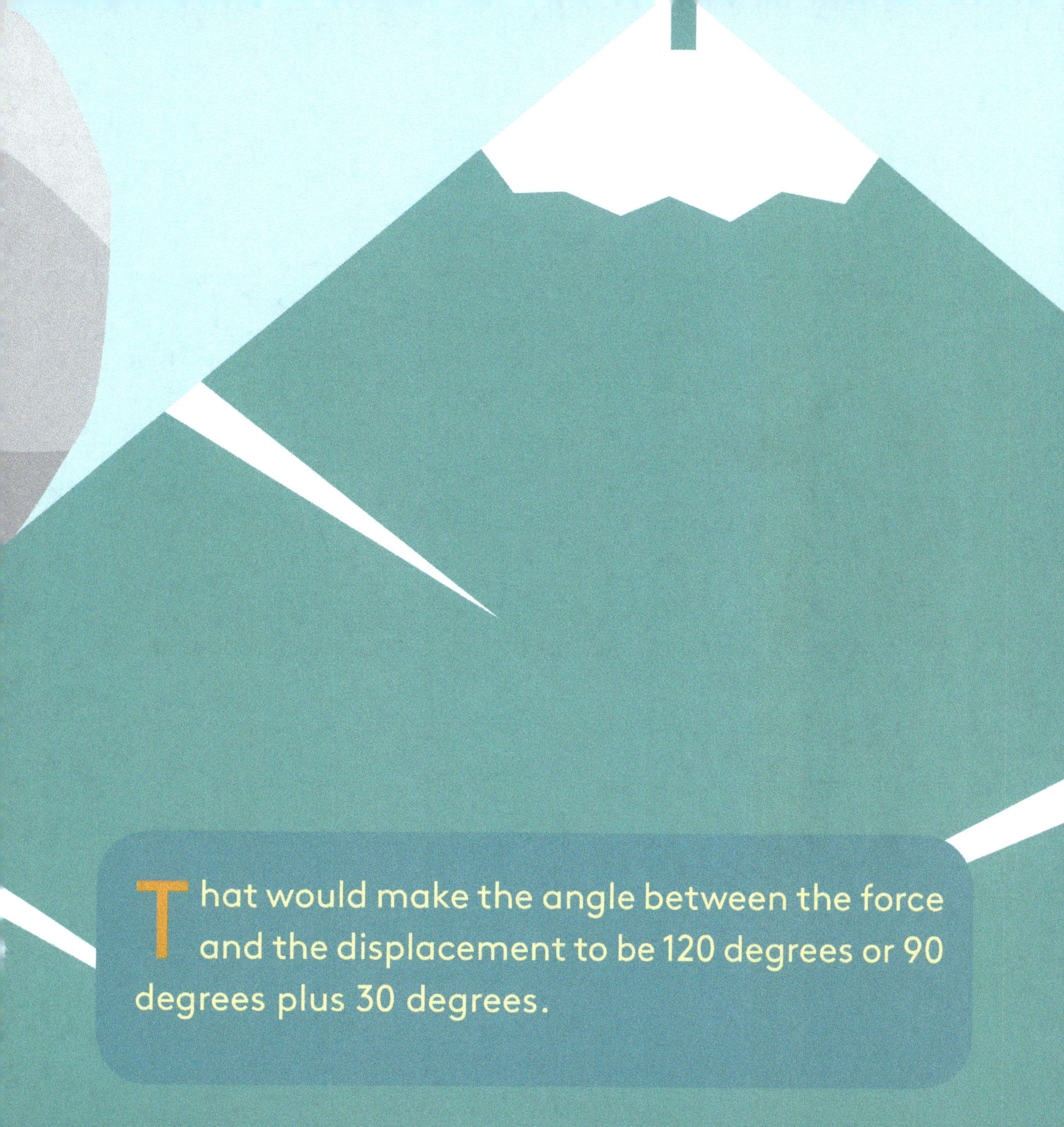
That would make the angle between the force and the displacement to be 120 degrees or 90 degrees plus 30 degrees.

W = 1 newton x 10 meters
x cos 120 degrees

Just to simplify, let's say the gravitational force is one newton and the displacement of the rock is 10 meters.

The formula would then be:

W = 1 newton x 10 meters x cos 120 degrees

FASCINATING FACTS ABOUT WORK

f your father is a physicist and all he does is read the computer screen all day, he isn't really working in terms of what "work" is meant in physics.

A foot-pound is another way that work is measured. One foot-pound is equivalent to approximately 1.36 joules.

Negative work is when the force that acts
on an object impedes its displacement.

E = mc²

Awesome! Now you know more about what work means in terms of physics. You can find more Physics books from Baby Professor by searching the website of your favorite book retailer.

Visit

BABY PROFESSOR
EDUCATION KIDS

www.BabyProfessorBooks.com
to download Free Baby Professor eBooks and view
our catalog of new and exciting Children's Books